DEDICATION

∞

I would like to dedicate this book to my mom and dad. Dad you have been a shining example of the image of manhood. You have always worked hard, cared for your family, and instilled godly values in all of us. Your wisdom is unparalleled and has guided me though some of the most difficult moments in my life. Your strength, tenacity, and care for people are the godly characteristics I admire the most. I pray that I make you half as proud as your son, as I am to call you "Dad."

Mom, your undying care and support are only rivaled by God's love for me. You have been a faithful cheerleader even in the games I lost in life. Thanks for pushing me to my destiny and never allowing me to settle. I didn't always see it, but now it is so clear. I would have never made it this far without you. May you reap one hundredfold of all that you have invested in me.

Co-Author

Tomi M. Ingram, Co-Author, is the founder and lead consultant of Associates of Promise, LLC the mission of which is to turn-around low-performing schools and their districts through research-based, continuous and sustainable improvements. She has worked over 30-years to empower and advance the lives of people of all ages to reach their destiny. As an educator, motivational speaker, political activist, and leader mentor, Ms. Ingram addresses critical issues that affect every aspect of human, professional, leadership, social, educational and spiritual development with a commitment to break the mindset of mediocrity, or worse, inferiority.

Snapshot of Skills...

You will be able to:

- Explore relevant topics that relate directly to components of life that will aide your understanding of yourself and the world around you.

- Identify and resolve conflict by problem solving and developing viable resolutions.

- Use active reading strategies to understand and extend your knowledge of what you read.

- Respond to what you read by thinking critically and using information to self-reflect and create change.

- Analyze significant themes and respond intelligently in a number of ways.

- Evaluate the attitudes, values and beliefs of others by making judgments and constructing ways to effect changes.

- Assess cause & effect relationships and draw conclusions regarding their impact.

- Formulate short answer and open-ended responses by pulling from text informaton to make relevant text-to-self, text-to-text, and text-to-world connections.

Things you should know:

✍ Respond in writing
🗣 Oral presentation
🕴 Flex your mental muscles and think critically

Read each chapter prior to engaging with workbook

WHAT COMES TO MIND WHEN YOU SEE THIS GUY?

Journal: Prior to reading the book reflect in writing on the following:

How are men defined in today's society?

_____
_____
_____

What factors are considered when defining men in today's society?

_____
_____
_____

Predict:

Looking at the cover of the book, brainstorm for 3-5 minutes on everything that comes to your mind while viewing the image. Be prepared to share your list with others.

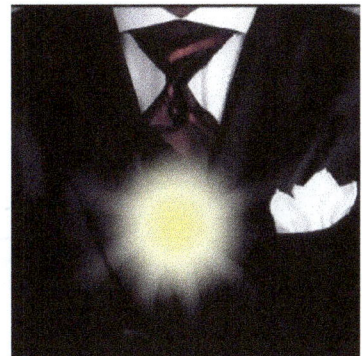

_____
_____
_____
_____
_____
_____
_____

✒ Based on both photos

- What did you assume about both men's characters while only having the picture to judge from?

  _____
  _____
  _____

- How does this exercise mirror real life? If so, in what ways?

  _____
  _____
  _____

- What can you do so that you are perceived in a more positive manner?

  _____
  _____
  _____

✒ Based on the title: **"Restoring the Male Image: a Look from the Inside Out"**

- In your opinion, are men in need of restoration?

  _____
  _____
  _____
  _____

- If so, in what areas or what ways?

  _____
  _____
  _____
  _____

- What is your definition of being a man?

  _____
  _____
  _____
  _____

- When does a boy become a man?

  _____
  _____
  _____
  _____

CHAPTER ONE

What Lies Beneath

✎ What does Henry Ward Beecher mean when he said "You and I do not see things as they are we see things as we are." What exactly is he implying to his audience?

_____
_____
_____

Would you agree with Dr. Ellis that "what people see creates a strong mental impression of who they think we are?" Explain. *(p.23)*

_____
_____
_____

✎ Who do people say that you are? What do others think of you? If others had to give an account of your life, what would they say? Use the character web below to record your comments. Use additional paper if needed.

Who would your FAMILY say you are?

_____
_____
_____
_____

Who would your TEACHER(S) say that you are?

_____
_____
_____
_____

Who do people say that you are?

Who would your FRIENDS say that you are?

_____
_____
_____
_____

Who would your NEIGHBORS say that you are?

_____
_____
_____
_____

Are you who others see you to be?   Explain your response in details.

_____
_____
_____
_____

✍ Write a rap or poem about "the hidden you" – the person behind the clothes, reputation, looks, and exterior. The "YOU" nobody sees, hears, understands, or knows.

_____
_____
_____
_____
_____
_____
_____
_____
_____
_____
_____
_____
_____
_____
_____
_____
_____
_____
_____
_____
_____
_____

✍ Evaluate the rap or poem you have just written and respond to the following:

Who are you?_____
_____
_____
_____

What feelings does the rap or poem evoke or bring to mind? _____
_____
_____
_____

Interpret the central ideas that you want to communicate in the rap/poem? _____
_____
_____
_____

Evaluate what is really important to you by examining your attitudes, beliefs, and values as they are expressed in the rap/poem? _____
_____
_____
_____
_____

What have you learned about yourself through this exercise? How does this reflective process benefit or not benefit you? _____
_____
_____
_____

1. Dr. Ellis shares his experience shopping for a watermelon. He said, "It looked good, and even sounded good, but there was something messed up inside...you can't judge anything based on its outward appearance alone." What is Dr. Ellis implying?

   _____

   _____

   _____

2. "And the two shall become one!"
   - What would happen if the "ME" everyone sees, is true to the "Me" I have inside?"

     _____

     _____

     _____

   - What would happen if you were on the outside was a true reflection of who you are on the inside?

     _____

     _____

     _____

1. What are your self-imposed limitations? In other words, what limitations have you placed on yourself?

   _____

   _____

   _____

2. What does it mean to "restore"one's self-esteem?

   _____

   _____

   _____

3. Using the following steps on page 27, write a reflection on how you can make your "internal a priority." Dig deep and discover the inner you!

   _____

   _____

   _____

   _____

   Create a list of any issues or conflicts you must begin to address.

   _____

   _____

   _____

   _____

- Take time and discover yourself and what's really in you. Be sure to record your results.

- Obtain an accountability partner, someone who will be honest with you and support you on your journey.

- Begin to love yourself and accept "all" of you. Track your changes and your approach.

- Focus on healing and growing on the inside more than dressing up the outside.

- Don't be afraid to seek outside help from others. Identify resourceful others and then respond to their counsel.

- Share your story with someone else in hopes that it would set you free from that which held you bound.

Tie It All In...*Page 28*

1. Does your image accurately reflect who you are? Why? Why not?

   _____

   _____

   _____

   _____

   _____

2. Have you gained a level of success in the eyes of other people but have a deep sense of failure or emptiness inside? Explain.

   _____

   _____

   _____

   _____

   _____

3. Describe the process you use to evaluate your personal motives.

   _____

   _____

   _____

   _____

   _____

4. Do you feel pressured to live up to the expectations of friends and family? If so, how do the expectations of others affect you? If not, how do you respond to the influences and/or expectations of others?

_____

_____

_____

_____

_____

5. How would you describe your relationships with others? Are they healthy and genuine, or are they toxic and lacking authenticity?

_____

_____

_____

_____

_____

6. Do you have a problem developing and maintaining intimate and/or close relationships? Explain.

_____

_____

_____

_____

_____

_____

CHAPTER TWO

VOCABULARY IN CONTEXT

Develop working definitions, examples and personal connections for each word.

Word	It means:	For example,	As it relates to my life…
self-esteem			
respect			
image			
restore			
compromise			
dignity			
integrity			
status quo			
character			
reputation			
habit			
self-reflection			
self-awareness			
perception			
judgment			

Restoring the Male Image: A Look from the Inside Out

Low-Self Esteem

What causes low self-esteem in men? How does the origin or cause of low self-esteem effect men if it is ignored? A **cause** is WHY something happens. An **effect** is WHAT happens. Show the cause and effect relationships using the chart below.

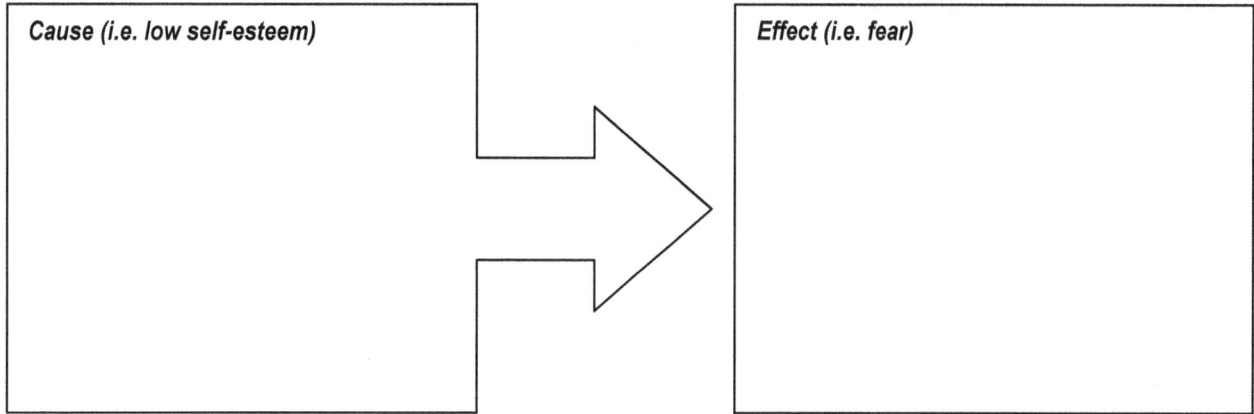

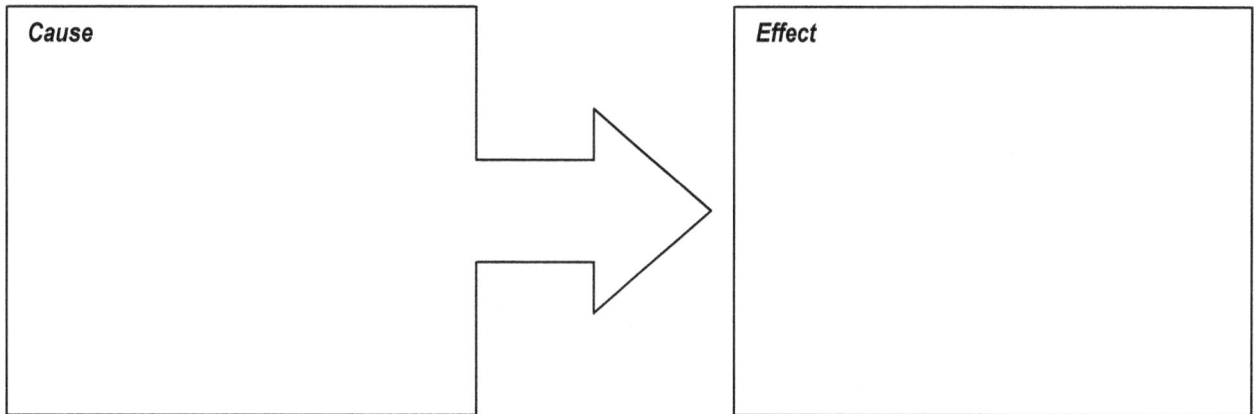

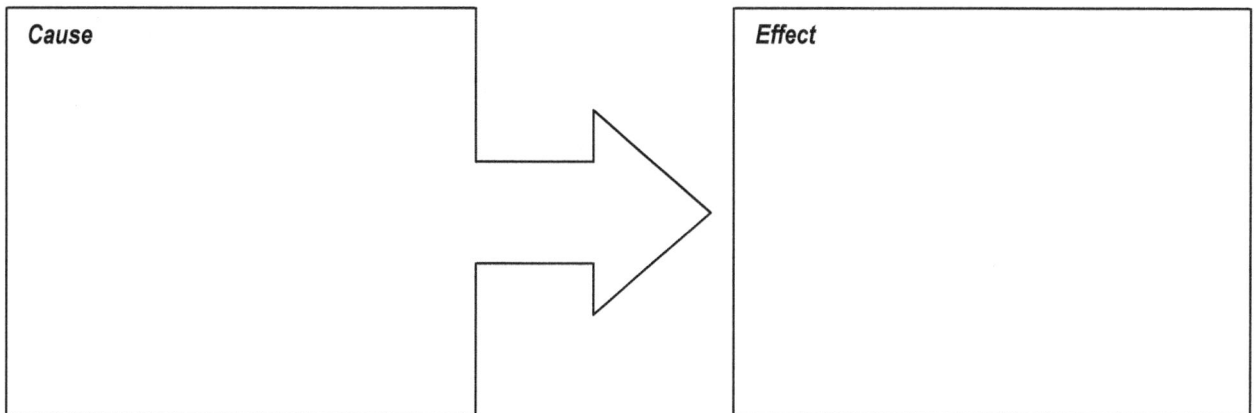

Cause (i.e. low self-esteem)	Effect (i.e. fear)

Cause	Effect

Cause	Effect

Page 33-36

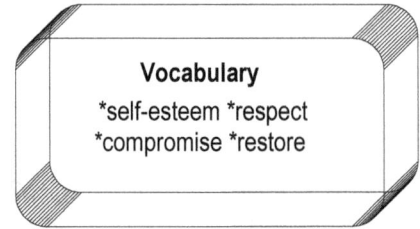

1. "Lack of self esteem is one of the biggest challenges facing our youth today, especially our black males. Dr. Suite stresses the importance of getting rid of the perception that young men must wear designer clothing to validate themselves, as name brands have a strong influence on young people's idea of image."

   In your opinion, is the above statement a perception, myth or reality?

   _____

   _____

   _____

   Is Dr. Suite correct in saying, "men must wear designer clothing to validate themselves?" Why? Why not?

   _____

   _____

   _____

2. ϒ Use the "Discussion Cards" on page 48 the following ways:

   • Imagine being nominated to represent your peers at the White House. Using Discussion Card #1 write a persuasive speech convincing delegates of the importance of investing in young people in America.

   • Read Discussion Card #2 and explain whether you agree or disagree with it. Give an example to support your response. Secondly, imagine you were asked to give advice to an audience of your peers, what two pieces of advice would you give to encourage them to be themselves.

   • Host a talk show in which you or a team of people will respond to Discussion Card #3. Who will your audience consists of? What questions will you ask? What counter arguments from audience participants would you anticipate?

   • Read the quote on Discussion Card #4. Interpret its meaning and give an example to support your response.

3. What is holding you back? What thoughts, comments, actions, events or people have caused you to think less of yourself?

   _____

   _____

   _____

   _____

✑Use the **Magnificent Me A-Z** chart in the back of your workbook and list positive attributes about yourself.

Tie It All In...*Page 36*

1. In what ways do you appreciate and celebrate your own accomplishments and good deeds? _____
    _____
    _____
    _____

2. Describe situations where you have experienced difficulty expressing your feelings? _____
    _____
    _____
    _____
    _____

3. Explain a time when you isolated yourself from other people and why?
    _____
    _____
    _____
    _____

4. Describe social settings in which you are initially shy and withdrawn? _____
    _____
    _____
    _____
    _____

5. How much effort do you put into friendships? Do you hold on to friendships (even bad ones) because you fear being alone, abandoned, other? Explain. _____
    _____
    _____
    _____
    _____

DIALOGUE WITH OTHERS

See what others think by using this page to interview them.
Record and share their responses with a friend.

Q What part do adults play in helping to bring an end to low self-esteem in young people?

A _____
_____
_____
_____

Q What contributions are you making towards the advancement of today's youth, young men in particular?

A _____
_____
_____
_____

Q How important is image and self-esteem to young men of today, especially the young black male?

A _____
_____
_____
_____

Q What are some challenges men are facing today?

A _____
_____
_____
_____

CHAPTER THREE

Imitations of Life

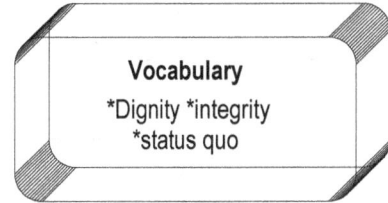

> **Vocabulary**
> *Dignity *integrity
> *status quo

Page 37-40

> *"The greatest difficulty is that men do not think enough of themselves, do not consider what it is that they are sacrificing when they follow in a herd, or when they cater for their establishment."* –Ralph Waldo Emerson, Poet, Essayist

✒ Read the above quote, what feelings does it evoke? What is the author trying to convey? Is the author's attitude in the above quote the same or different from you own?

_____
_____
_____
_____
_____
_____
_____

1. How far are you willing to go to keep up with the "status quo?"

_____
_____
_____

2. How important is it for you to "fit in" and be accepted by others?

_____
_____
_____

3. What does it mean to have dignity?

_____
_____
_____

4. What is integrity? Would you consider yourself to be a person of great dignity and integrity? Provide a rationale for your answer.

_____
_____
_____

1. Dr. Ellis writes " In the long run, if you continue chasing after the 'in crowd' you will end up surrounded by people who love you for what you have as opposed to genuinely loving you for who you are." What is Dr. Ellis implying? Which would you prefer genuine relationships or those predicated on how I look on the outside?

   _____

   _____

   _____

   _____

   _____

2. What does the quote great Shakespearean quote, "To thy own self be true," mean to you?

   _____

   _____

   _____

3. Can you feel when you are comprising who you are to fit in with others? What do you do when you get that feeling?

   _____

   _____

   _____

4. Dr. Ellis said "You can lead a life full of all of the trappings of success, but if you never fulfill your purpose, your life is in vain?" Fulfilling your purpose is the key ingredient to attaining wholeness. Discuss.

   _____

   _____

   _____

5. How is purpose fulfilled?

   _____

   _____

   _____

6. What steps are you going to put in place to ensure that your purpose in life is realized?

   _____

   _____

   _____

7. Have you attracted people as Dr. Ellis said, based on your outward appearance but still feel empty within?

   _____

   _____

   _____

8. What unhealthy relationships have you settled for? What actions are you willing to take to dismiss harmful relationships to allow room for more wholesome ones?

_____

_____

_____

9. Who is your role model?

_____

_____

_____

10. Why do you admire that person?

_____

_____

_____

11. What qualities do you emulate of that person?

_____

_____

_____

Tie It All In...*Page 40*

1. Do you feel the need for approval from others? Why? Why not?

_____

_____

_____

2. How do you respond to criticism? Are your actions beneficial or harmful to you?

_____

_____

_____

3. Do you find yourself wearing particular clothing because of others as opposed to your own style?

_____

_____

_____

4. How would you describe yourself - a follower or a trail blazer? Explain your response.

_____

_____

_____

CHAPTER FOUR

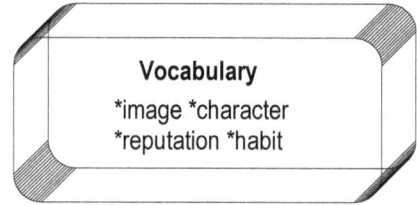

Vocabulary
*image *character
*reputation *habit

Page 43-47

1. Do you agree or disagree with Bixler's comment, "Your image transmits a message about you all day - every day. There is no erase button." Why? Why not?

   _____
   _____
   _____
   _____

2. What does your image say to the world?

   _____
   _____
   _____
   _____

3. Are you being perceived in respect to who you really want to be? Explain.

   _____
   _____
   _____
   _____

4. What reputation has owned you?

   _____
   _____
   _____
   _____

5. Dr. Ellis says, "Everything about you becomes your brand." What brand have you become?

   _____
   _____
   _____
   _____

Having a good reputation is critical! However, your reputation may have been marred by a wrong decision, act or deed. The good news is "**FAILURE IS WRITTEN IN PENCIL.**"

✎Using a pencil, write down all of the mistakes, failures, and errors that you have made in your past. Write down your good, your bad, and your ugly. Then, using the biggest eraser you can find, **ERASE! ERASE! ERASE IT ALL** as a sign of starting anew - start to create a prouder you. Forgetting those things that are behind you and with everything you can muster, press forward to those things that are before you and **BECOME!**

_____
_____
_____
_____
_____
_____
_____
_____
_____
_____
_____
_____
_____
_____
_____
_____
_____
_____
_____
_____
_____
_____
_____
_____
_____
_____
_____
_____
_____
_____

1. It takes a life time to build a reputation but only a second to damage it. Moving forward, what are you going to do to improve your character and ultimately your reputation?

    _____
    _____
    _____

2. What is it that you want to do with your life?

    _____
    _____
    _____

3. What are you good at? Spend time and discover your gifts and talents. Write them down.

    _____
    _____
    _____

4. Describe a time when you may have been misinterpreted or misunderstood?

    _____
    _____
    _____

5. What measures might you take to ensure that people understand who you are and who you are striving to be?

    _____
    _____
    _____

6. What does man's external image say about him?

    _____
    _____
    _____

✎ What does "image" mean to you?

- Voza Rivers describes image as "an extension of who we are."
- Lloyd Boston said, "image is a total consciousness of my being."
- Tye Tribbett: "Image means perception."
- Clyde Wilder: "Image is looking good and being a complete package."
- Mark Provost: "Image embodies the being of a person."

Image means: _____
_____
_____
_____

Survey ten people on the following questions and see how you measure up in the sight of others. Analyze their responses and use them as a guide to self-reflect.

- o What message does my image give you?
- o What do my clothes say to you about who I am?
- o What impressions do you have when you see me?

Tie It All In...*Page 47*

1. How much time do you spend on your personal appearance? Do you think you need to spend more or less time? Why?

_____

_____

_____

_____

2. What message do you intend for your clothes to convey about you? Explain if you are satisfied or displeased with what is being communicated.

_____

_____

_____

_____

3. Do people compliment you on your clothing? How often?

_____

_____

_____

_____

4. Do you have a business suit? If not, how long will it take for you to invest in one?

_____

_____

_____

_____

✎ "The challenge with reputation is that it is often formulated by what you allow people to see." What have you allowed people to see of you? What is the latest news reported about you? Write a third-person editorial about yourself.

1. Explain the saying "Your reputation precedes you so always strive for perfection." In what way might you relate to this quote?

_____
_____
_____
_____
_____

2. "Character differs from reputation in that it goes deeper than who people perceive you to be, but reveals who you really are inside." Spend some time assessing your character.

- What is your personality like _(the combination of your qualities that makes you who you are)_ ?

_____
_____
_____
_____

- What are your temperaments _(your very nature as it permanently effects your behavior)_?

_____
_____
_____
_____

- How would you describe your disposition _(attitude, mood or qualities of mind)_?

_____
_____
_____
_____

H. Jackson Brown Jr. makes the claim that, "Our character is what we do when we think no one is looking." If so, what have you been doing? If the walls around you could speak, what would they utter? Write your response here.

_____
_____
_____
_____
_____
_____
_____
_____
_____
_____

✏ "Habit is something that a person is known to do routinely, without much thoughts."
Use the T-chart to list all of your good habits on one side and bad habits on the other to
determine if the good outweighs the bad.

Weighing The Cost

GOOD HABITS	BAD HABITS

Restoring the Male Image: A Look from the Inside Out

Tie It All In...*Page 50*

1. Do you think your reputation accurately reflects your character? Why or why not?

    _____
    _____
    _____
    _____
    _____

2. What have you done to create the reputation you have right now?

    _____
    _____
    _____
    _____
    _____

3. What have you done to maintain your reputation?

    _____
    _____
    _____
    _____
    _____

4. Will most people praise your character or say unfavorable things about you? Why?

    _____
    _____
    _____
    _____
    _____

5. What bad habits are you willing to work on?

    _____
    _____
    _____
    _____
    _____

CHAPTER FIVE

I.M.A.G.E

✎How do you measure up with Dr. Ellis' definition of IMAGE? Where do you rate yourself on a scale of 1-5 with five being an area of strength and one an area of weakness?

5 = Very Strong   4 = Strong   3 = Average   2 = Needs improvement   1 = Weak

I.M.A.G.E CHECK

	Where I am!	Where I want to be!	How I will work on it!	Tracking my progress!
INTEGRITY				
MANHOOD				
AUTHORITY				
GENEROSITY				
EXCELLENCE				

✎If "Integrity, like character is who you are when no one else is looking," who are you? Can what you do in secret be seen in the light? Who are you when no one else is around?

_____
_____
_____
_____
_____
_____

How are you being true to yourself? "Integrity says I will not try to fool people with a polished exterior. A man desires to be pure in who he is and what he does, so that the external presentation is just a reflection of his internal state. Therefore, integrity can be seen as being true to oneself."

With that in mind, does your external honestly reflect your internal? Are you true to who you are?

_____
_____
_____
_____
_____
_____
_____
_____
_____

Tie It All In...*Page 53*

1. How do you know that you are a man of your word?

   _____
   _____
   _____
   _____

2. Are you the same person in public as you are in private? Explain.

   _____
   _____
   _____
   _____

3. How do you respond in situations when decisions are made which conflict with your moral values?

   _____
   _____
   _____
   _____

4. How do you hold yourself personally accountable for your actions? Or do you?

   _____
   _____
   _____
   _____

I DARE YOU!

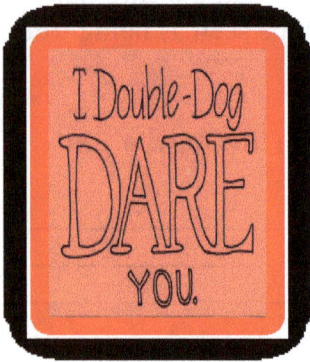

it! For too long, we have dwelt upon the dim reality of absentee athers, lack of male presence, and the shortage of positive male ole models.

DARE YOU to seek out men who are visionaries, leaders, eachers, cultivators, providers and protectors. Don't wait for them o appear – find them.

command you to move beyond your comfort zone and position yourself ful others. If they don't adopt you - adopt them.

✍**Reciprocate the process!** Be the change you want to see by mentoring or spending time with a boy in your family, community, school, or church. Give what you wished you had received. If each one, teach one, imagine how powerful such a domino effect would be in the restoration of men as these stages of development are reciprocated. After all, role models are key! In the words of Dr. Maya Angelou, "As you learn - teach, as you get - give."

You are being called to make a difference. What are some things you will do?

_____
_____
_____
_____
_____
_____
_____
_____
_____
_____

✍ In Chapter One, the question was posed, "What is a man?" Has your opinion changed after reading the section on M=Manhood? Explain.

_____
_____
_____
_____
_____
_____
_____
_____
_____
_____

✎ "Manhood is a responsibility. It is ownership and accountability for your actions at all times."
How do you measure up to Dr. Ellis' definition of manhood?

_____
_____
_____
_____
_____
_____
_____

✎ Dr. Ellis wants to compel you to take time for self inspection to re-evaluate whether or not
you are a man of integrity. Not whether you 'look' like an honest man, but that you truly are a
man who posses personal ethics. How will your life change to ensure that your desire to become
a man of integrity is a reality?

_____
_____
_____
_____
_____
_____
_____
_____
_____

✎The three goals I will commit to working on to improve my life in the area of integrity are...

1. _____
   _____
   _____

2. _____
   _____
   _____

3. _____
   _____
   _____

✎ Recognizing those who help to shape aspects of our lives gives us a better understanding of who we are. For example, from your association with others you can determine why we act the way we do …your temperament, habits, addictions, ambitions, etc. Who do you find yourself most emulating or acting like?

_____
_____
_____
_____
_____
_____
_____

✎Identify those who have shaped your life and those who have made a difference. Then, find a way to simply say "Thank You" for being a significant component in your development.

Be mindful, not all of your influences may be positive. The goal is to sharpen your awareness of your strengths and weakness, generational bondage and hereditary assets as you aspire to become a new creation. Face life – don't turn your back on it.

Jot down, how are you going to say thank you? *(email, card, handwritten letter, phone call, tweet…)*

_____
Name

_____
Name

Thank you

Tie It All In..._page 59_

1. Who was your first male role model?

   _____
   _____
   _____

2. Did you ever thank that person for impacting your life? If yes, how? If no, why not?

   _____
   _____
   _____
   _____

3. Young men are in need of approachable male role models. Do you mentor young men in your church, community, or family?

   _____
   _____
   _____
   _____

4. As a young man, have you identified a role model and determined why they fit the bill? If so, explain.

   _____
   _____
   _____
   _____

5. Having trouble identifying role models? Research men of the past and present who meet the criteria which you seek. Allow aspects of their lives, ethics, and conducts provide a model for you.

   _____
   _____
   _____
   _____

You have heard it said more than once or twice, "No one owes you anything."
As a man of authority - you create opportunities even if they don't exist.
You cannot give up or throw in the towel.
That's Just Not What Men Do!!

Tie It All In...*page 61*

1. How do the people under your authority respect you?

_____
_____
_____

2. How do the people under you follow you? Is it by fear or admiration?

_____
_____
_____

3. When you speak, do others listen?

_____
_____
_____

What you make happen for someone else,
God will make happen for you!
BECOME A GIVER!
Start small and be generous!
Philanthropy is important.

Tie It All In*...page 62*

1. How often do you find yourself focusing on the needs of others? In what ways can you help to improve someone else's situation?

_____
_____
_____

2. Do you donate money or assets to a charity, community, or church?

_____
_____
_____

3. How will you volunteer your time as a mentor, coach, tutor, etc?

_____
_____
_____

≈ "Excellence is the drive for a life above average." How do you live a life above the norm? How would living with a consciousness to do your very best improve the quality of your life and your relationships?

_____
_____
_____
_____
_____

≈ What is the author implying when he says: "Excellence is an attitudinal decision… a level of personal accountability without supervision."

_____
_____
_____
_____
_____

Tie It All In… *page 63*

1. Identify three areas in your life that you can sharpen? How you intend on sharpening each area?

   a) _____
   _____
   _____

   b) _____
   _____
   _____

   c) _____
   _____
   _____

2. How would you describe your attention to detail?

   _____
   _____
   _____

3. Explain how you go the extra mile on projects, in relationships, etc

   _____
   _____
   _____

4. How do you intend to start putting your best foot forward in all that you do?

   _____
   _____
   _____

CHAPTER SIX

TAKE ME BACK

Evaluate and Explain

🎙Imagine you had to give the keynote address to a group of aspiring young men such as yourself. Using key points Dr. Ellis raises regarding the Harlem Renaissance, what would you say? Write your speech and then challenge yourself by sharing it with someone who would benefit from it.

_____

_____

_____

_____

_____

_____

_____

_____

_____

_____

_____

_____

_____

_____

🎙History can be our greatest teacher. As Dr. Ellis points out. "The Harlem Renaissance brought an awareness of culture and pride to people." How might that awareness of culture and pride inspire your community and peers today? In what way can you honor the legacy and sacrifice others made for you in order for your life to be better?

_____

_____

_____

_____

_____

_____

_____

_____

_____

_____

_____

_____

_____

_____

How might your generation use the following themes to awaken youth to impact societal affairs, drive issues in politics, increase educational and communal accountability, and maintain personal responsibility?

> ➢ Internal Pride
> ➢ Perseverance
> ➢ Overcoming Obscurity
> ➢ Purpose - Driven Mindsets

_____
_____
_____
_____
_____
_____
_____
_____
_____
_____
_____
_____
_____
_____
_____
_____
_____
_____

Renaissance is about making a new start, establishing a new beginning, recovering, and revitalizing. What would be the advantages and disadvantages of having a 21st century renaissance movement in your community, and ultimately in the United States of America?

_____
_____
_____
_____
_____
_____
_____
_____
_____
_____
_____
_____
_____
_____

Think and Respond

✍Use the Venn diagram below to compare the Harlem Renaissance to the 21ˢᵗ century? Discuss the similarities and differences but more importantly, what can we learn from each.

✍During his historical speech President Barack Obama declared, "It's time for a change!" What change was he referring to? In what sense did his campaign help raise the consciousness of America toward a revival of pride?

_____

_____

_____

_____

_____

_____

_____

_____

_____

_____

_____

REPRESENT! "Today we have the freedom to come and go as we please and we leave our homes with no consciousness of who we represent. We must still be mindful that not only do we represent ourselves, but our families and our people."

Think about your family heritage and cultural roots. How well do you represent them?

_____
_____
_____
_____
_____
_____
_____
_____

- Are you the same on the street as you would be with your grandparents, teacher, or pastor?

_____
_____
_____
_____
_____

- Are you guilty of using profanity with no regard or respect for those around you (adults, senior citizens, or children)?

_____
_____
_____
_____
_____

- Is indecent exposure okay with you and, therefore, you find wearing your pants below your waist, revealing your underwear and rear end to be of no offense to others?

_____
_____
_____
_____
_____

How well do you represent? Are you pleased or would you be ashamed? Would you teach your children to mimic your ways or would you encourage them to take a different route?   Write a 3-5 page essay or produce a short film in response to the above.

FilmStrip

Based on the excerpt below, write an expository essay explaining what does being a "Renaissance Man" mean to you and how might one become a Renaissance Man?

"Being a Renaissance Man is not a destination, it's a lifestyle. It's a way of life. It's the way you think. It's not a period. A Renaissance Man is always in process, always evolving. He never arrives and parks. He always maintains the posture of a student, willing to learn about different cultures, ideas and traditions. The world is always evolving and changing and if the world is changing, you have to as well. But maintaining the right image should be constant.

_____
_____
_____
_____
_____
_____
_____
_____
_____
_____
_____
_____
_____
_____
_____
_____
_____
_____
_____
_____
_____
_____
_____

✎Let's talk about PRIDE! Like the movie, Beauty and The Beast, pride has two sides, it can be positive or negative. If you are not careful as to its victory or venom, you will war constantly with the good you want to do and the wrong you're ultimately doing.

TUG-OF-WAR

PRIDE (-)		PRIDE (+)
Arrogant		Pleasant
Smug		Delightful
Conceited		Self-respect
Self-important		Honorable
Snobby		Dignified
Self-righteous		Self-esteem

- Which side of pride are you on?

  _____
  _____
  _____
  _____

- Which side will you allow to win?

  _____
  _____
  _____
  _____

- How quick are you to prove a point? How eager are you to learn?

  _____
  _____
  _____
  _____

- Do you think you know it all? Or are you teachable – okay doing what's right?

  _____
  _____
  _____
  _____

- Are you marked with an aroma of dignity and charm or vanity and conceit?

_____
_____
_____
_____

✍ "Men from the Harlem Renaissance were intrinsically motivated and driven not just for themselves but for their families and moreover, their communities.   What motivates men of today? What tangible things are men doing to advance their families and neighborhoods?

_____
_____
_____
_____
_____
_____
_____
_____
_____
_____
_____
_____
_____
_____
_____
_____

🎤Imagine having the opportunity to stand before Barack Obama, the 44th President of the United States of America at one of his town hall meetings on behalf of your generation. What would you say with respect to your collective (1) accomplishments; (2) interests; and (3) needs?

_____
_____
_____
_____
_____
_____
_____
_____
_____
_____
_____
_____

CHAPTER SEVEN

THE POWER OF THE MEDIA

Propaganda is an array of communication techniques used to influence others by persuading them to buy into an idea, product, program, movement, interest group, and etc. Two forms in particular are Bandwagon and Celebrity Appeal. Celebrity appeal suggests because a "celebrity" endorses a product, stands behind an event, or spear-heads a movement "everyone else" should follow. After all, if they are behind it, it must be good. Bandwagon suggests that what is offered is "so good" that "everyone else" is doing it, therefore, so should you.

Design a Power Point presentation on the effects of propaganda in the media and its influences on consumers.

The heart of economics is based primarily on two factors. One is "Supply" and the other is "Demand." As long as consumers show a demand for a product via their interest, purchases and buying decisions, industry leaders will continue to supply - to meet consumer needs. For example, if there's a demand for white-tee's and wife beaters, regardless of their lack of personality and appeal, such items will continue to dominant clothing stores thereby providing little or no clothes that depict character and class.

Consumers vs. Merchants! Your assignment is to organize a youth rally, parent meeting or community round table discussing the power of supply and demand. Encourage them to come together to raise their expectations of what the next generation should wear by demanding more quality, variety, decency and pride in what is supplied by merchants especially within the inner city. Knowing that consumers have the power to effect change by demanding what is good, excellent and acceptable will influence what is provided.

Pretend you are a columnist writing for your local newspaper or magazine. Run a month long series titled "The Buying Decisions of the Consumer." What factors do we consider before purchasing? What motivates or attracts the buyer to a particular product? Feel free to explore your own topics or select from those below. Furthermore, challenge yourself by sending your best pieces to leading publishers.

1. Monkey See! Monkey Do!
2. Subliminal Messages
3. Bandwagon and Celebrity Appeal
4. Propaganda and Media Impact
5. Fads vs. Fame
6. Impacts of Buying Decisions
7. Right Motives and Wrong Apparel
8. First Impressions

What is the author implying when he says, "It is easy to become enthralled with the aspects of someone else's life and believe you will have the happiness celebrities appear to have?"

In what ways do we "accept the media's concept of image as the standard and spend our lives in an attempt to look and live like them?"

Utilize text-to-self; text-to-text; text-to-world connections to support your response.

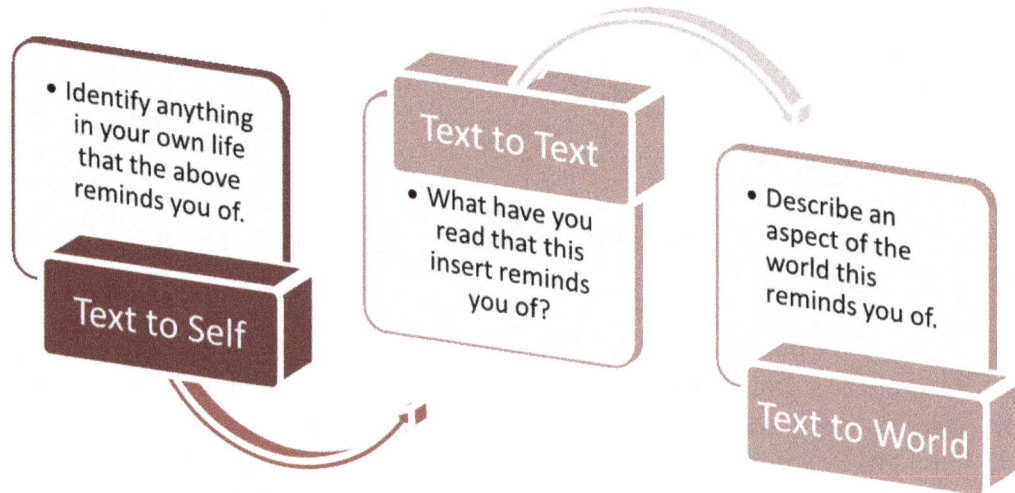

- Identify anything in your own life that the above reminds you of.

Text to Self

Text to Text

- What have you read that this insert reminds you of?

- Describe an aspect of the world this reminds you of.

Text to World

Text to Self _____
_____
_____
_____
_____
_____
_____

Text to Text _____
_____
_____
_____
_____
_____
_____

Text to World _____
_____
_____
_____
_____
_____
_____

Take Inventory! Do you have classic pieces and timeless articles that are essential to every man's wardrobe or is your closet filled with "Trendy" apparel that is in style today and unbefitting tomorrow?

WARDROBE INVENTORY

Garment	#	Colors	Condition (good, fair, poor)	Wear to:
Ex. Jeans	10	10-Blue, 2-Black	Fair, worn-out	School, game..
KHAKIS				
JEANS				
SLACKS				
SUITS				
T-SHIRTS				
POLO SHIRTS				
DRESS SHIRTS				
SWEATERS				
BLAZERS				
SWEATS				
HOODIES				
TIES				
CUFF LINKS				
POCKET SQUARES				
SNEAKERS				
SHOES				
BOOTS				
OTHER:				

Restoring The Male Image: A Look From The Inside Out

Based on Dr. Ellis' "Dressing For All Occasions" What areas of your wardrobe need improvement? _____

_____

_____

_____

_____

DISCUSSION CARDS

Use Discussion Cards 1-4 to complete lessons on page 12 of your interactive workbook.

"Communities must instill enough confidence inside of our youth so that when their standards are being compromised they have the fortitude to stand on their own."

(1)

"Young people must be careful not to assimilate because it is what everyone else is doing. Otherwise their true identity will succumb to society's pressure to replicate its image, as opposed to being their own unique self."

(2)

"Today's youth have to find their true identity through parents, role models, teachers and self discovery."

(3)

"The moment you alter your perception of yourself and your future, both you and your future begins to change."

(4)

Magnificent Me A-Z

A _____

B _____

C _____

D _____

E _____

F _____

G _____

H _____

I _____

J _____

K _____

L _____

M _____

N _____

O _____

P _____

Q _____

R _____

S _____

T _____

U _____

V _____

W _____

X _____

Y _____

Z _____

POST – READING ACTIVITIES

Take some time and think about all that you have learned by reading *Restoring the Male Image: A Look From the Inside Out*. How has your life changed as a result of working through the text? What impression has the content made upon you? Use the chart below to assess your life before reading the book and after the book. Record specific events you encounter to bring about a better you.

Before Reading **Life Changing Events** **After Reading**

1. _____
   _____
   _____
   _____
   _____

2. _____
   _____
   _____
   _____
   _____

3. _____
   _____
   _____
   _____
   _____

4. _____
   _____
   _____
   _____
   _____

5. _____
   _____
   _____
   _____
   _____

CONNECTING THE DOTS

Assess how your life has changed in the areas specified below. Coordinate a point in each box to rate how much you have matured in each area and/or those areas where immaturity still exists. Lastly, connect each point to form a create line graph that will help you to visualize your changes.

	Image	Reputation	Self-esteem	Integrity	Authority	Manhood	Generosity	Excellence
Mature								
5								
4								
3								
2								
1								
Immature								

1. By looking at the line graph above, my strongest points of growth are:

   _____

   _____

   _____

2. The steps I took to mature in the above areas were:

   _____

   _____

   _____

3. By looking at the line graph points I need to improve:

   _____

   _____

   _____

   _____

4. Steps I will put into action to develop areas I have yet to mature are:

   _____

   _____

   _____

   _____

Problem and Solution

Identify two problem areas of your life that need your attention. Then brainstorm possible solutions you're willing to try to resolve them.

Problem

Solution

Solution

Solution

Problem

Solution

Solution

Solution

ϒ I challenge you to get the word out!
Social Media is a powerful way to raise the awareness and awaken the consciousness of people.

There are so many young people waiting for leaders like you to call them to action. I challenge you to use the platform of social media to give your generation something to connect and tie themselves to, and that being - GREATNESS!

- Share your story with the world.

- Celebrate your progress and milestones to encourage others.

- Share before and after pictures, thoughts and stories.

- Create a 30 second public service announcement.

- Instagram your journey to DrAlex and others.

- Make the best of 140 characters by tweeting https://twitter.com/TiedToGreatness.

- Follow Tied to Greatness on Facebook: https://www.facebook.com/TiedToGreatness.

- Connect groups and like minded organizations to your face book and twitter to inspire others as yourself.

- Educate others as to how they may take action, influence their community, and make a difference.

Take the Survey

The TIED TO GREATNESS™ team would like to take this time and thank you for your participation in the recent Tied To Greatness Assembly. Your attendance was not only appreciated by the team, but also by the young men who you had a chance to interact with.

As we continue to spread this initiative to other cities, it is important that we hear from you to make certain that what we are doing is relevant and is making an positive impact on the young men.

http://www.tiedtogreatness.org/survey/

Visit the website to learn more: http://www.TiedToGreatness.com
You Tube: www.youtube.com/watch?v=WBytQ-eRx5A

I Want To Hear From You

Dr. Alex Dr. Ellis
P.O. Box 1062
New Brunswick, NJ 08901
DrAlex@tiedtogreatness.org.
http://www.tiedtogreatness.org/survey/

Author, Dr. Alexis Ellis wants to hear your feedback, progress, life changing discoveries as a result of embracing and implementing vital aspects of this book. What was most important to you? Would you be interested in participating in Tied To Greatness events?

Date: _____

Dear Dr. Dr. Ellis:

_____
_____
_____
_____
_____
_____
_____
_____
_____
_____
_____
_____
_____
_____
_____
_____
_____

Respectfully Submitted,

_____
Your Name

Why Tied to Greatness Now?

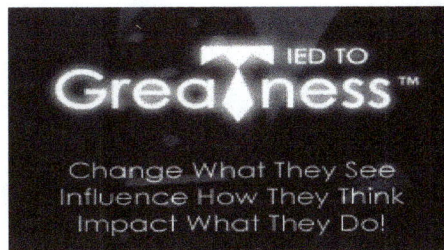

Change the present outlook and statistical predictions!

Why Tied to Greatness™ Now?

According to the U.S. Census Bureau in 2011, for the first time in history, the majority of babies born in the U.S. were babies of color. Thus, in the not too distant future, the viability of our country's communities, labor force and democracy will largely be shaped and predicated on the opportunities we provide for those children.

How are we, as a country, doing?

- Nationally, only 52% of Black males and 58% of Latino males graduate from high school in four years, while 78% of White, non-Latino males graduate in four years. *(The Schott 50 State Report on Public Education and Black Males. September 2012)..*

- In 38 of the 50 states and the District of Columbia, Black males have the lowest graduation rates among Black, Latino and White, non-Latino male and female participants. *(The Schott 50 State Report on Public Education and Black Males. September 2012)..*

- While states and districts have been able to provide supports to secure a timely high school diploma for over three-quarters of White, non-Latino males, only a little more than half of Black and Latino males were provided with the same supports. *(The Schott 50 State Report on Public Education and Black Males. September 2012).*

- Black and Hispanic participants represent more than 70 percent of those involved in school-related arrests or referrals to law enforcement. *Department of Education 2012.*

- Nationwide, African-Americans represent 26% of juvenile arrests, 44% of youth who are detained, 46% of the youth who are judicially waived to criminal court, and 58% of the youth admitted to state prisons. *NAACP Center on Juvenile and Criminal Justice.*

- 85% of children who show behavioral disorders, 71% of high school dropouts and 85% of all youths in prison come from fatherless homes. *The Boys Initiative.*

Visit the website to learn more: http://www.TiedToGreatness.com

Help us take this mission of changing and empowering the lives of inner city young men all across this nation by telling a friend; becoming a volunteer, mentor, sponsor, and being an active participant in a city near you. For more information visit our website at www.TiedToGreatness.org